POLAND:
TAP

DISCOVERING THE TREASURES OF CENTRAL EUROPE

SHARON E. WENGER

Copyright © 2024 [Sharon E. Wenger]

All rights reserved. No part of this publication may be reproduced, distributed, or transmitted in any form or by any means, including photocopying, recording, or electronic or mechanical methods, without the prior written permission of the author, except in the case of brief quotations embodied in critical reviews and certain other noncommercial uses permitted by copyright law.

TABLE OF CONTENT

1. Introduction to Poland
2. Planning Your Trip
3. Warsaw: The Heart of Poland
4. Kraków: A Medieval Gem
5. Wrocław: A City of Bridges
6. Gdańsk: A Baltic Sea City
7. Poznań: A City of Festivals
8. The Tatra Mountains: Poland's Natural Beauty
9. The Baltic Coast: Poland's Seaside Treasures
10. Białowieża Forest: A UNESCO World Heritage Site
11. Polish Cuisine: A Taste of Central Europe
12. Polish Culture and Traditions
13. Poland for Solo Travelers
14. Poland for Couples
15. Poland for Families: Kid-Friendly Travel in 2024
16. Budget and Costs

Introduction to Poland

Poland, a country steeped in history and culture, offers a unique and unforgettable travel experience. With its stunning landscapes, charming cities, and warm hospitality, Poland has something to offer everyone. From the medieval grandeur of Kraków to the modern vibrancy of Warsaw, there's always something to discover.

- **A Brief History:**

Poland's history is a rich and complex tapestry, shaped by centuries of political turmoil and cultural exchange. The country's medieval past is evident in its many historic cities and castles, while the 20th century saw Poland endure great hardship, including World War II and the Cold War. Despite these challenges, Poland has emerged as a resilient and vibrant nation.

- **Cultural Overview:**

Polish culture is a blend of Slavic, Germanic, and Latin influences. Music, literature, and art have played a significant role in shaping Poland's identity. The country is renowned for its folk music, traditional dances, and exquisite craftsmanship. Polish cuisine, with its hearty and flavorful dishes, is another important aspect of the country's culture.

Why Visit Poland?

There are many reasons why Poland is a must-visit destination. Here are a few:

- **Stunning Landscapes:** Poland boasts a diverse range of landscapes, from the majestic Tatra Mountains to the pristine Baltic Sea coast.

- **Historical Cities:** Poland's cities, such as Kraków, Warsaw, and Wrocław, offer a fascinating glimpse into the country's past.

- **Rich Culture:** Poland's culture is vibrant and diverse, with something to appeal to all interests.

- **Friendly People:** Poles are known for their warmth and hospitality, making visitors feel welcome and at home.

- **Affordable Travel:** Poland is a relatively affordable destination, making it a great choice for budget-conscious travelers.

Planning Your Trip

Poland, with its rich history, stunning landscapes, and vibrant culture, offers a unique and unforgettable travel experience. To ensure a smooth and enjoyable trip, careful planning is essential. This guide will provide you with valuable information on various aspects of planning your Polish adventure.

When to Visit:
The best time to visit Poland depends on your preferences and interests. Spring (April to June) and autumn (September to October) are generally considered the most pleasant seasons, with mild temperatures and fewer crowds.

Summer (July and August) is peak tourist season, with longer days and warmer weather, but also higher prices and larger crowds. Winter (December to February) offers a magical atmosphere with snow-covered landscapes, but can be very cold, especially in the northern regions.

Getting There:
Poland is well-connected to other European countries and has several international airports, including Warsaw Chopin Airport, Kraków-Balice Airport, and Gdańsk Lech Wałęsa Airport. You can fly directly to Poland from many major cities worldwide. Alternatively, you can take a train or bus from neighboring countries.

Visas and Immigration:
Most visitors to Poland do not need a visa if they are staying for less than 90 days. However, it's essential to check the specific visa requirements for your nationality before you travel. You may need to present your passport, proof of accommodation, and return ticket when entering Poland.

Currency and Costs:
The Polish złoty (PLN) is the national currency. You can exchange money at banks, currency exchange offices, and ATMs. The cost of living in Poland is generally lower than in many Western European countries, making it a budget-friendly destination. However, prices in tourist areas can be higher.

Accommodation:
Poland offers a wide range of accommodation options to suit all budgets and preferences. Hotels, hostels, apartments, and guesthouses are available in major cities and popular tourist destinations. Booking accommodation in advance, especially during peak season, is recommended.

Transportation:
Poland has an efficient public transportation system, including trains, buses, and trams. Trains are a convenient and affordable way to travel between major cities. Buses are also a good option for shorter distances. Within cities, public transportation is well-developed, with frequent services and affordable fares.

Language and Culture:

Polish is the official language of Poland, but English is widely spoken in tourist areas. Learning a few basic Polish phrases can be helpful and show respect for the local culture. Poland has a rich cultural heritage, with a strong tradition of music, art, and literature. Be respectful of local customs and traditions.

Packing List:

When packing for your trip to Poland, consider the season and the activities you plan to do. Essential items include comfortable clothing, appropriate footwear, a raincoat, and a camera. If you're planning to hike in the mountains, pack warm clothing and sturdy hiking boots.

Safety:

Poland is generally a safe country for travelers. However, it's always important to be aware of your surroundings and take precautions to protect yourself. Avoid carrying large amounts of cash or valuables, and be cautious when using ATMs.

Warsaw: The Heart of Poland

Warsaw, the capital of Poland, is a city that pulsates with a unique blend of history, culture, and modernity. Once devastated by World War II, Warsaw has risen from the ashes to become a vibrant and cosmopolitan metropolis. Its charming Old Town, bustling city center, and rich cultural scene make it a must-visit destination for any traveler exploring Poland.

A Historic Gem:

Warsaw's Old Town (Stare Miasto) is a UNESCO World Heritage Site that has been meticulously rebuilt after its destruction during World War II. The cobblestone streets, colorful buildings, and charming squares transport visitors back to medieval times. The Royal Castle, a symbol of Poland's history, is a must-see attraction. Inside, visitors can admire the opulent interiors, including the Grand Hall and the Royal Chapel.

Another iconic landmark in Warsaw is the Palace of Culture and Science (Pałac Kultury i Nauki), a towering skyscraper built by the Soviet Union during the Communist era. Today, the building houses a variety of cultural institutions, including theaters, museums, and cinemas. Visitors can take an elevator to the observation deck for panoramic views of the city.

A Vibrant Metropolis:
Beyond its historic attractions, Warsaw is a bustling metropolis with a thriving cultural scene. The city center is filled with trendy shops, cafes, and restaurants. The Nowy Świat street is a popular pedestrian zone lined with shops, boutiques, and street performers. For a taste of local life, visit the Hala Koszyki, a modern food hall with a variety of cuisines and bars.

Warsaw also offers a vibrant nightlife scene. The city is home to numerous bars, clubs, and live music venues. The Praga district, once a working-class neighborhood, has become a popular destination for nightlife enthusiasts.

Cultural Experiences:

Warsaw is a city rich in cultural experiences. The National Museum houses a vast collection of Polish art, including works by famous artists like Jan Matejko and Józef Chełmoński. The Chopin Museum is dedicated to the life and work of the renowned Polish composer. For a unique cultural experience, visit the Lazienki Park, a beautiful palace complex surrounded by gardens and lakes.

Day Trips:
Warsaw is a great base for exploring other parts of Poland. The nearby town of Otwock is known for its sanatoriums and spa resorts. The historic city of Toruń, the birthplace of astronomer Nicolaus Copernicus, is also worth a visit. For a more adventurous day trip, consider exploring the Białowieża Forest, a UNESCO World Heritage Site home to bison and other wildlife.

Warsaw is a city that offers something for everyone. Whether you're interested in history, culture, or simply enjoying a vibrant metropolis, Warsaw is sure to leave a lasting impression.

Kraków: A Medieval Gem

Kraków, Poland's former capital, is a city steeped in history and culture. With its well-preserved medieval design, vibrant atmosphere, and rich artistic heritage, Kraków offers a truly enchanting experience.

A Walk Through History:
The heart of Kraków is the Market Square (Rynek Główny), one of the largest medieval market squares in Europe. Surrounded by colorful guild houses, the square is a bustling hub of activity, with street performers, cafes, and restaurants. At the center of the square stands the Cloth Hall (Sukiennice), a Gothic building that once housed a bustling textile market. Today, the Cloth Hall is home to a variety of shops and art galleries.

One of the most iconic landmarks in Kraków is Wawel Castle, a hilltop fortress that has served as the residence of Polish kings for centuries. The castle complex includes the Royal Cathedral, where many Polish monarchs are buried, and the Wawel Hill, which offers stunning panoramic views of the city.

Kazimierz: A Jewish Quarter:
Kraków's Jewish Quarter, Kazimierz, is a charming neighborhood with a rich history. During the Holocaust, Kazimierz was the center of the Kraków ghetto. Today, the neighborhood has been revitalized and is a popular destination for tourists. Visitors can explore the Old Synagogue, one of the oldest synagogues in Poland, and visit the Galicia Jewish Museum, which tells the story of Jewish life in Kraków.

A Cultural Hub:

Kraków is a city with a thriving cultural scene. The city is home to numerous theaters, museums, and galleries. The National Museum in Kraków houses a vast collection of Polish art, including works by famous artists like Jan Matejko and Józef Chełmoński. The Jagiellonian University, one of Europe's oldest universities, is also located in Kraków.

A Culinary Delight:

Kraków is a foodie's paradise, with a wide variety of restaurants offering everything from traditional Polish cuisine to international fare. Some of the must-try dishes in Kraków include: pierogi (dumplings), bigos (a hearty stew), and żurek (sour rye soup). For a unique dining experience, visit one of the many bars and pubs in Kazimierz.

Day Trips:

Kraków is a great base for exploring other parts of Poland. The nearby town of Wieliczka is home to the Wieliczka Salt Mine, a UNESCO World Heritage Site that has been operating for over 700 years. Visitors can take a guided tour of the mine and marvel at the intricate salt carvings.

Another popular day trip from Kraków is to Auschwitz-Birkenau, a former Nazi concentration camp. The camp is a sobering reminder of the horrors of the Holocaust. Visitors can tour the camp and learn about the tragic history of this place.

Kraków is a city that offers something for everyone. Whether you're interested in history, culture, or simply enjoying a vibrant atmosphere, Kraków is sure to leave a lasting impression.

Wrocław: A City of Bridges

Wrocław, a charming city located in southwestern Poland, is often referred to as the "City of Bridges" due to its numerous crossings over the Odra River and its tributaries. With its picturesque architecture, vibrant cultural scene, and friendly atmosphere, Wrocław is a captivating destination for travelers.

A City of Bridges:
The Odra River, which flows through the heart of Wrocław, is spanned by numerous bridges, each with its own unique character. One of the most iconic bridges is the Tumski Bridge, which connects the Old Town with the Cathedral Island. The bridge offers stunning views of the river and the historic buildings on both sides.

Another notable bridge is the Most Piaskowy, a pedestrian bridge that is illuminated at night, creating a magical atmosphere.

A Historic Gem:
Wrocław's Old Town (Stare Miasto) is a UNESCO World Heritage Site that boasts beautiful architecture, cobblestone streets, and charming squares. The Old Town Hall, a Gothic building with a clock tower, is a prominent landmark. The Market Square (Rynek) is another must-see attraction, with its colorful guild houses and vibrant atmosphere.

The Cathedral Island (Wyspa Katedralna) is another historic area of Wrocław. The island is home to the St. John the Baptist Cathedral, a Gothic masterpiece with a towering spire. Visitors can also explore the nearby Bishop's Palace and the Museum of the Archdiocese of Wrocław.

A Cultural Hub:

Wrocław is a city with a thriving cultural scene. The ciy is home to numerous theaters, museums, and galleries. The National Museum in Wrocław houses a vast collection of Polish art, including works by famous artists like Jan Matejko and Józef Chełmoński.

The Wrocław Opera House is another cultural gem, offering a variety of performances throughout the year.

Wrocław is also known for its vibrant music scene. The city hosts numerous music festivals, including the Wrocław Opera Festival and the Wrocław Jazz Festival.

A Student City:

Wrocław is a university city with a large student population. This contributes to the city's lively atmosphere and diverse cultural scene. There are many student bars, cafes, and restaurants in Wrocław, making it a great place to experience the city's youthful energy.

Day Trips:

Wrocław is a great base for exploring other parts of Poland. The nearby town of Świdnica is home to the Church of Peace, a UNESCO World Heritage Site that was built in the 17th century. The historic city of Zgorzelec, located on the border with Germany, is also worth a visit.

Wrocław is a city that offers something for everyone. With its beautiful architecture, vibrant culture, and friendly atmosphere, Wrocław is a must-visit destination for travelers exploring Poland.

Gdańsk: A Baltic Sea City

Gdańsk, a city located on the Baltic Sea coast of Poland, boasts a rich history dating back to the 10th century. As a prominent member of the Hanseatic League, Gdańsk played a significant role in European trade during the Middle Ages. Its strategic location on the Baltic Sea made it a vital hub for commerce and cultural exchange.

The city's historical significance was further cemented by its pivotal role in the Solidarity movement, a pivotal force in the downfall of communism in Poland. The shipyard where the movement was founded is now a UNESCO World Heritage Site, serving as a poignant reminder of the city's courageous struggle for freedom.

A Coastal Gem:

Gdańsk's coastal location offers a wealth of natural beauty and recreational opportunities. The city's Old Town, a UNESCO World Heritage Site, is a picturesque area characterized by colorful buildings, cobblestone streets, and a vibrant atmosphere. The Artus Court, a Gothic building that once served as a meeting place for merchants, is a prominent landmark.

The Baltic Sea coast provides a picturesque backdrop for a variety of outdoor activities. Visitors can enjoy swimming, sunbathing, and water sports at the nearby beaches, including Sopot, Poland's most famous seaside resort. The Hel Peninsula, located at the tip of the Hel Spit, offers stunning coastal scenery and opportunities for nature observation.

A Cultural Hub:

Gdańsk is a city with a thriving cultural scene, boasting many theaters, museums, and galleries. The National Museum in Gdańsk houses a vast collection of Polish art, including works by renowned artists like Jan Matejko and Józef Chełmoński. The Polish Baltic Philharmonic, a renowned cultural institution, offers a diverse range of classical music performances.

The city's vibrant music scene is another highlight. Gdańsk hosts numerous music festivals, including the Gdańsk Shakespeare Festival and the Gdańsk Summer Opera Festival, showcasing a variety of artistic expressions.

Day Trips:

Gdańsk serves as an excellent base for exploring other fascinating destinations along the Baltic Sea coast. The nearby town of Sopot, known for its long wooden pier, is a popular seaside resort offering a range of attractions. The city of Hel, located at the tip of the Hel Peninsula, is a nature lover's paradise, with its pristine beaches, birdwatching opportunities, and unique maritime atmosphere.

Poznań: A City of Festivals

Poznań, a charming city located in western Poland, is renowned for its vibrant atmosphere, rich history, and lively cultural scene. With its well-preserved medieval Old Town, stunning architecture, and numerous festivals, Poznań offers a unique and unforgettable travel experience.

A Medieval Gem:
The heart of Poznań is the Old Town Square (Stary Rynek), one of the largest medieval market squares in Europe. Surrounded by colorful guild houses, the square is a bustling hub of activity, with street performers, cafes, and restaurants. At the center of the square stands the Town Hall (Ratusz), a Gothic building with a famous astronomical clock that features a procession of figures every hour.

One of the most iconic landmarks in Poznań is the Imperial Castle (Zamek Cesarski), a fortress built in the 16th century. Today, the castle houses the National Museum and offers stunning panoramic views of the city.

A City of Festivals:

Poznań is known as a "city of festivals" due to its vibrant cultural scene and numerous events throughout the year. One of the most popular festivals is the International Poznan Fair (Międzynarodowe Targi Poznańskie), one of the largest trade fairs in Central Europe. The fair attracts visitors from all over the world and showcases a wide range of products and services..

Another popular festival is the Saint Martin's Day Parade (Święto Marcina), a colorful event that takes place on November 11th. The parade features hundreds of people dressed as Saint Martin, as well as floats, marching bands, and horse-drawn carriages.

Other notable festivals in Poznań include the Easter Fair (Jarmark Wielkanocny), the Saint John's Day Fair (Jarmark św. Jana), and the Poznań Jazz Festival.

A Culinary Delight:

Poznań is a foodie's paradise, with a wide variety of restaurants offering everything from traditional Polish cuisine to international fare. Some of the must-try dishes in Poznań include pierogi (dumplings), bigos (a hearty stew), and żurek (sour rye soup). For a unique dining experience, visit one of the many bars and pubs in the Old Town.

Day Trips:
Poznań is a great base for exploring other parts of Poland. The nearby town of Gniezno, the first capital of Poland, is a historic city with a beautiful cathedral and a well-preserved Old Town. The city of Toruń, the birthplace of astronomer Nicolaus Copernicus, is another popular day trip destination.

Poznań is a city that offers something for everyone. With its vibrant atmosphere, rich history, and lively cultural scene, Poznań is a must-visit destination for travelers exploring Poland.

The Tatra Mountains: Poland's Natural Beauty

The Tatra Mountains, a majestic mountain range on the border between Poland and Slovakia, are a must-visit destination for nature lovers and outdoor enthusiasts. With their towering peaks, pristine lakes, and diverse wildlife, the Tatras offer a breathtaking and unforgettable experience.

A Majestic Mountain Range:

The Tatra Mountains are the highest mountain range in the Carpathian Mountains, with Rysy (2,503 meters) being the highest peak. The Polish Tatras are divided into the High Tatras (Tatry Wysokie) and the Western Tatras (Tatry Zachodnie). The High Tatras are known for their rugged terrain, towering peaks, and stunning glacial valleys. The Western Tatras, on the other hand, offer a more gentle landscape with rolling hills, meadows, and forests.

Hiking and Trekking:

The Tatra Mountains are a paradise for hikers and trekkers. There are hundreds of trails that cater to all levels of experience, from easy walks to challenging climbs. Some of the most popular hiking trails include the Morskie Oko, a glacial lake surrounded by breathtaking scenery, and the Orla Perć, a demanding ridge trail that offers panoramic views of the mountains.

Winter Sports:

The Tatra Mountains are also a popular destination for winter sports enthusiasts. The ski resorts of Zakopane and Kościelisko offer a wide range of slopes, from beginner-friendly to expert-level. Visitors can also enjoy snowboarding, cross-country skiing, and snowshoeing in the mountains.

Wildlife and Nature:
The Tatra Mountains are home to a diverse range of wildlife, including chamois, deer, wolves, and bears. The forests are also home to a variety of bird species, including eagles, owls, and woodpeckers. Visitors can spot wildlife by hiking through the mountains or taking a guided tour.

A Cultural Experience:
The Tatra Mountains are also a cultural destination. The town of Zakopane, located at the foot of the mountains, is known for its unique highland culture. Visitors can experience the local traditions by attending folk music concerts, watching traditional dances, or visiting the Tatra Museum.

Day Trips:

The Tatra Mountains are a great base for exploring other parts of Poland. The nearby town of Nowy Targ is a historic market town with a charming Old Town. The city of Kraków, Poland's former capital, is also a popular day trip destination from the Tatras.

The Tatra Mountains are a must-visit destination for anyone who loves nature and outdoor activities. With their breathtaking scenery, diverse wildlife, and rich cultural heritage, the Tatras offer a truly unforgettable experience.

The Baltic Coast: Poland's Seaside Treasures

Poland's Baltic Sea coast offers a stunning blend of natural beauty, historical charm, and vibrant seaside resorts. With its sandy beaches, picturesque fishing villages, and unique coastal landscapes, the Baltic coast is a must-visit destination for travelers seeking relaxation, adventure, and cultural experiences.

Sandy Beaches and Seaside Resorts:
The Baltic Sea coast is home to numerous sandy beaches that are perfect for swimming, sunbathing, and water sports. Some of the most popular seaside resorts include Sopot, Kołobrzeg, and Mielno. Sopot is known for its long wooden pier, which is the longest in Europe, while Kołobrzeg offers a wide range of spa and wellness facilities. Mielno is a family-friendly resort with a beautiful sandy beach and a lively atmosphere.

Picturesque Fishing Villages:
Along the Baltic coast, you'll find charming fishing villages with colorful houses, narrow streets, and a traditional way of life. Jastarnia, Władysławowo, and Łeba are just a few examples of these picturesque villages. Visitors can explore the local markets, sample fresh seafood, and enjoy the peaceful atmosphere of these coastal communities.

Unique Coastal Landscapes:
The Baltic coast offers a variety of unique coastal landscapes. The Hel Peninsula, a narrow strip of land that stretches into the Baltic Sea, is a popular destination for nature lovers. Visitors can hike or bike along the peninsula's trails, visit the lighthouse at Hel, and observe birdlife in the nearby nature reserve.

The Slowinski National Park, located in the northern part of the Baltic coast, is another must-see destination. The park is known for its moving sand dunes, which are among the highest in Europe. Visitors can hike through the dunes, explore the coastal forests, and spot various bird species.

Cultural Experiences:
The Baltic coast is also rich in cultural experiences. The cities of Gdańsk and Gdynia, located on the coast, offer a wealth of historical and cultural attractions. Visitors can explore the historic Old Towns, visit museums and galleries, and enjoy the vibrant nightlife scene.

The Baltic coast is a popular destination for music festivals and cultural events. The Sopot International Song Festival, one of the most prestigious music contests in Europe, takes place annually in Sopot. Other popular events include the Gdańsk Shakespeare Festival and the Gdynia Film Festival.

Day Trips:
The Baltic coast offers many opportunities for day trips. Visitors can explore the nearby cities of Toruń and Bydgoszcz, which are known for their historic Old Towns and cultural attractions. The city of Szczecin, located in the far north of Poland, is another interesting destination with a rich maritime history.

The Baltic coast is also a must-visit destination for travelers seeking a combination of relaxation, adventure, and cultural experiences. With its stunning beaches, picturesque villages, and unique coastal landscapes, the Baltic coast offers something for everyone.

Białowieża Forest: A UNESCO World Heritage Site

Białowieża Forest, a vast primeval forest located in eastern Poland and western Belarus, is one of the last remaining remnants of the ancient European wilderness. Renowned for its biodiversity and ecological significance, Białowieża Forest was declared a UNESCO World Heritage Site in 1992.

A Primeval Wilderness:
Białowieża Forest is one of the largest and oldest lowland forests in Europe, dating back thousands of years. The forest is home to a diverse range of plant and animal species, many of which are rare or endangered. The forest's unique ecosystem is a result of its undisturbed state, which has allowed it to retain its natural character.

Biodiversity Hotspot:

Białowieża Forest is a biodiversity hotspot, with over 800 species of vascular plants, 250 species of birds, and 60 species of mammals. One of the most iconic species found in the forest is the European bison, the largest land mammal in Europe. Other notable species include the wolf, lynx, elk, and brown bear.

The forest is also home to a variety of rare and endangered plants, including the European white hellebore, the marsh marigold, and the sundew. The forest's diverse flora and fauna are a testament to its ecological significance.

Conservation Efforts:

Białowieża Forest has been the subject of extensive conservation efforts for many years. In the 19th century, the Russian Tsar Alexander II established a protected area in the forest to preserve the European bison. Since then, various conservation initiatives have been implemented to protect the forest's biodiversity and ecosystem.

In recent years, the forest has faced threats from logging and infrastructure development. However, conservationists have fought to protect the forest and ensure its survival for future generations.

A Cultural Landscape:

Białowieża Forest is not only an ecological treasure but also a cultural landscape. The forest has been inhabited by humans for centuries, and its history is intertwined with the local culture. The forest has been a source of inspiration for artists, writers, and musicians.

Visitors to Białowieża Forest can learn about the forest's history and culture by visiting the Białowieża National Park Visitor Centre and the Museum of Nature and Forestry.

A Must-Visit Destination:

Białowieża Forest is a must-visit destination for nature lovers and anyone interested in conservation. The forest offers a unique opportunity to experience the beauty and diversity of the European wilderness. Visitors can hike through the forest's trails, observe wildlife, and learn about the forest's rich history and culture.

Białowieża Forest is a testament to the importance of protecting our planet's natural heritage. By preserving forests like Białowieża, we can ensure the survival of countless species and maintain the delicate balance of our planet's ecosystems.

Polish Cuisine: A Taste of Central Europe

Polish cuisine is a delightful blend of flavors, textures, and traditions that reflect the country's rich history and cultural influences. With its hearty dishes, hearty soups, and delicious pastries, Polish food offers a unique and satisfying culinary experience.

Hearty and Satisfying Dishes:
One of the most iconic Polish dishes is pierogi, a type of dumpling filled with savory or sweet ingredients. Popular fillings include meat, cheese, sauerkraut, and potatoes. Pierogi are typically served with butter, sour cream, or onions.

Another popular Polish dish is bigos, a hearty stew made with sauerkraut, meat (usually pork, beef, or sausage), mushrooms, and spices. Bigos is often simmered for hours, allowing the flavors to meld together.

Other traditional Polish dishes include żurek, a sour rye soup topped with a boiled egg and sausage; kotlet schabowy, a breaded pork cutlet; and golonka, a pork knuckle braised in beer or sauerkraut.

Hearty Soups:

Polish cuisine is known for its delicious soups, which are often served as a main course. Barszcz, a beet soup, is a classic Polish dish with a vibrant red color and a tangy flavor. It is often served with dumplings or sour cream. Rosół, a chicken noodle soup, is another popular Polish soup, known for its comforting and flavorful broth.

Delicious Pastries:

Polish pastries are renowned for their sweetness and richness. Pączki, deep-fried doughnuts filled with jam or cream, are a popular treat, especially during Carnival. Mazurek, a traditional Polish cake, is often enjoyed during Easter and other special occasions. It is typically made with a shortcrust pastry base and topped with a variety of fillings, including poppy seed, chocolate, and fruit.

Regional Specialties:
Polish cuisine varies from region to region, with each region having its own unique specialties. In the southern region of Galicia, one can find hearty dishes like kopytka (potato dumplings) and obwarzanek krakowski (a traditional Kraków bread roll). In the northern region of Pomerania, seafood dishes like smoked fish and herring are popular.

Cultural Influences:
Polish cuisine has been influenced by a variety of cultures, including German, Lithuanian, and Ukrainian. This is evident in the use of ingredients and cooking techniques that are common in these regions. For example, the use of sauerkraut and spices like marjoram and cumin is a reflection of Polish cuisine's Germanic influences.

A Culinary Adventure:
Polish cuisine offers a unique and satisfying culinary adventure. With its hearty dishes, delicious soups, and sweet pastries, Polish food is sure to delight even the most discerning palate. Whether you're a seasoned traveler or a newcomer to Polish cuisine, you're sure to find something to enjoy.

Polish Culture and Traditions

Poland, a country steeped in history and culture, offers a unique and fascinating glimpse into Central European traditions. From its vibrant folklore to its rich artistic heritage, Polish culture is a tapestry of diverse influences and enduring customs.

Folklore and Customs:
Polish folklore is rich in myths, legends, and superstitions. One of the most famous Polish folk tales is the legend of the mermaid, a mythical creature said to inhabit the Vistula River. Other popular folk tales feature witches, dragons, and other fantastical creatures.

Polish customs and traditions are deeply rooted in the country's history and religion. One of the most important Polish holidays is Easter, celebrated with colorful eggs, traditional meals, and religious ceremonies. Christmas is another significant holiday, marked by the exchange of gifts, family gatherings, and the singing of carols.

Music and Dance:
Music and dance have played a vital role in Polish culture for centuries. Polish folk music is characterized by its lively rhythms and use of traditional instruments such as the violin, accordion, and flute. Popular folk dances include the mazurka, polonaise, and krakowiak.

Poland has also produced many world-renowned classical composers, including Frédéric Chopin, Ignacy Paderewski, and Karol Szymanowski. The Chopin Museum in Warsaw is dedicated to the life and work of the famous composer.

Art and Literature:
Polish art and literature have a long and distinguished history. The country has produced many famous painters, sculptors, and writers. Jan Matejko, Józef Chełmoński, and Jacek Malczewski are among the most renowned Polish painters. Famous Polish writers include Adam Mickiewicz, Henryk Sienkiewicz, and Bruno Schulz.

Language and Etiquette:
Polish is a Slavic language with a rich vocabulary and complex grammar. While English is widely spoken in tourist areas, learning a few basic Polish phrases can be helpful and show respect for the local culture.

Polish people are generally friendly and hospitable. It is customary to greet people with a handshake and to maintain eye contact during conversations. When visiting a Polish home, it is polite to remove your shoes at the door.

Religious Beliefs:
The majority of Poles are Roman Catholic, although there are also significant minorities of Orthodox Christians and Protestants. Religion plays a significant role in Polish culture and society. Many Polish customs and traditions are rooted in religious beliefs.

Polish culture is a rich and diverse tapestry that reflects the country's history, traditions, and influences. From its vibrant folklore to its rich artistic heritage, Polish culture offers a unique and fascinating experience. By understanding Polish culture and traditions, visitors can gain a deeper appreciation for this beautiful and fascinating country.

Poland for Solo Travelers

Poland is a welcoming and safe country that is also a great destination for solo travelers. With its friendly people, beautiful landscapes, and rich history, Poland offers a unique and unforgettable experience.

Solo Travel Tips:

- Learn a few basic Polish phrases: This will show respect for the local culture and make your trip more enjoyable.

- Stay in hostels or guesthouses: These accommodations are often more social and offer opportunities to meet other travelers.

- Join a group tour or activity: This is a great way to meet other people and explore the country.

- Be aware of your surroundings: As with any destination, it's important to be aware of your surroundings and take precautions to protect yourself.

Solo-Friendly Destinations:

- **Warsaw:** The capital city of Poland is a vibrant and cosmopolitan city with a wide range of attractions and activities.

- **Kraków:** This historic city is a popular destination for solo travelers, with its charming Old Town, beautiful architecture, and lively atmosphere.

- **Wrocław:** This charming city is known for its picturesque canals, colorful buildings, and vibrant cultural scene.

Solo-Friendly Accommodations:

- **Hostels:** Hostels are a great option for solo travelers, as they offer affordable accommodation and opportunities to meet other people.

- **Guesthouses:** Guesthouses are often smaller and more intimate than hotels, and they can offer a more personalized experience.

- **Apartments:** Renting an apartment can be a good option for solo travelers who prefer more privacy and independence.

Poland for Couples

Poland offers a romantic and enchanting setting for couples seeking a memorable getaway. From historic cities and stunning landscapes to charming villages and cozy retreats, there's something for every couple to enjoy.

Romantic Getaways:

- **Warsaw:** The capital city of Poland offers a romantic blend of history, culture, and modern amenities. Explore the charming Old Town, take a romantic boat ride on the Vistula River, or enjoy a candlelit dinner at a cozy restaurant.

- **Kraków:** This historic city is a popular destination for couples seeking a romantic getaway. Stroll through the charming Market Square, visit Wawel Castle, or take a horse-drawn carriage ride through the city.

- **Gdańsk:** The Baltic Sea coast offers a romantic and relaxing atmosphere. Enjoy a beach walk, take a boat tour, or visit the charming fishing villages of the region.

- **Tatra Mountains:** For a truly romantic getaway, head to the Tatra Mountains. Hike through the stunning scenery, enjoy a cozy mountain retreat, or take a romantic cable car ride.

Honeymoon Destinations:

- **Zakopane:** This mountain resort town is a popular honeymoon destination, offering breathtaking scenery, romantic accommodations, and plenty of outdoor activities.

- **Białowieża Forest:** This ancient forest is a peaceful and secluded retreat, perfect for couples seeking a romantic and relaxing getaway.

- **Sopot:** This seaside resort town offers a romantic atmosphere, beautiful beaches, and a variety of activities for couples.

Romantic Accommodations:

- **Boutique Hotels:** Poland has many charming boutique hotels that offer a romantic and intimate atmosphere.

- **Spa Resorts:** Indulge in a relaxing spa treatment at one of Poland's many spa resorts.

- **Countryside Retreats**: Escape to the countryside and enjoy a peaceful and romantic getaway at a charming country house or manor.

Poland for Families: Kid-Friendly Travel in 2024

Poland offers a delightful blend of history, culture, and natural beauty, making it an ideal destination for a family vacation. With its charming cities, stunning landscapes, and a variety of kid-friendly attractions, Poland is sure to create lasting memories for families of all ages.

Kid-Friendly Attractions:

- **Zoos and Aquariums:** Poland boasts several excellent zoos and aquariums that are perfect for families with young children. The Warsaw Zoo and the Gdańsk Zoo both offer a wide range of animal exhibits and educational programs. For a marine adventure, visit the Oceanarium in Sopot, where you can explore underwater tunnels and see a variety of fascinating sea creatures.

- **Amusement Parks:** Energylandia, Poland's largest amusement park, is a must-visit for families with thrill-seeking children. With its thrilling roller coasters, water rides, and other attractions, Energylandia offers fun for the whole family. Smaller amusement parks like Park Dinozatorów in Bałtow and Park Miniatur in Toruń are also great options for families with younger children.

- **Children's Museums:** Poland has several interactive museums that are perfect for curious kids. The Copernicus Science Centre in Warsaw offers hands-on exhibits on science, technology, and the natural world. The Museum of Technology in Kraków is another great option for families with children interested in science and engineering.

Family-Friendly Activities:

- **Hiking and Biking:** Poland's beautiful countryside offers many opportunities for family-friendly hiking and biking. The Tatra Mountains are a great place for a family hike, with trails suitable for all ages and abilities. The Baltic Sea coast is perfect for bike rides, with scenic routes and beautiful coastal views.

- **Castle Visits:** Poland is home to many historic castles that are perfect for a family outing. Wawel Castle in Kraków, Malbork Castle, and Czocha Castle are all worth visiting.

Boat Tours: Take a boat tour on the Vistula River in Warsaw or the Odra River in Wrocław. This is a great way to see the city from a different perspective and enjoy a relaxing day out.

Family-Friendly Accommodation:

- **Hotels:** Many hotels in Poland offer family-friendly amenities such as connecting rooms, children's menus, and play areas.

- **Resorts:** Resorts like the Aqua-Park in Tarnowskie Góry and the Polana Szymoszkowa in Zakopane offer a wide range of family-friendly activities and accommodations.

- **Apartments:** Renting an apartment can be a great option for families with young children, as it provides more space and flexibility.

Tips for Traveling with Kids in Poland:

- **Plan Ahead:** Research family-friendly attractions and activities before your trip.

- **Pack Essentials:** Don't forget to pack essentials like sunscreen, insect repellent, and comfortable shoes.

- **Be Flexible:** Children can be unpredictable, so be prepared to adjust your plans as needed.

- **Take Breaks:** Schedule breaks throughout the day to rest and recharge.

- **Enjoy the Experience:** Most importantly, have fun and make lasting memories with your family!

Poand offers a wonderful and unforgettable experience for families. With its diverse attractions, beautiful landscapes, and friendly people, Poland is sure to create lasting memories for you and your family.

Budget and Costs for Your Trip

Currency:
The official currency of Poland is the Polish Złoty (PLN). You can exchange currency at banks, currency exchange offices, and ATMs. It's generally a good idea to exchange a small amount of currency upon arrival and withdraw more as needed.

Cost of Living:
Poland is generally a budget-friendly destination compared to many Western European countries. However, prices can vary depending on the city and tourist season. Accommodation, food, and transportation are generally more affordable outside of major cities and during the off-peak season.

Accommodation:
Accommodation costs in Poland vary widely depending on the type of accommodation, location, and season. Hostels are the most budget-friendly option, followed by guesthouses and apartments. Hotels can be more expensive, especially in popular tourist destinations during peak season.

Food and Drinks:
Eating out in Poland can be affordable, especially if you stick to local eateries and avoid touristy areas. Street food, such as pierogi and zapiekanki, is a great way to save money. Alcohol, especially beer, is relatively inexpensive in Poland.

Transportation:
Public transportation in Poland is generally affordable. Trains are a convenient and cost-effective way to travel between major cities. Buses are also a good option for shorter distances. Within cities, public transportation is well-developed, with frequent services and affordable fares.

Activities and Attractions:
The cost of activities and attractions in Poland varies depending on the type of activity and the location. Museums, galleries, and historic sites often have entrance fees. Outdoor activities like hiking and biking are generally free, but you may need to pay for equipment rentals.

Tips for Saving Money:

- **Travel during the off-season:** Prices for accommodation, flights, and activities are generally lower during the off-peak season (shoulder seasons and winter).

- **Stay in hostels or guesthouses:** These are often more affordable than hotels.

- **Cook your own meals:** Eating out can add up quickly, so consider cooking your own meals in your accommodation or buying groceries and preparing picnics.

- **Use public transportation:** Public transportation is generally affordable in Poland.

- **Take advantage of free activities:** There are many free things to do in Poland, such as walking tours, visiting parks, and enjoying the local atmosphere.

Sample Budget:

Here is a sample daily budget for a solo traveler in Poland:
- Accommodation: €20-€40
- Food: €15-€25
- Transportation: €5-€10
- Activities and Attractions: €10-€20

This budget can be adjusted depending on your travel style and preferences. By following these tips and planning ahead, you can enjoy a memorable trip to Poland without breaking the bank.

Printed in Great Britain
by Amazon